BROKEN BEFORE THE STORM

BOOKS BY C. PIERRE-RUSSELL

Sheila the Shy Shark

Save the Missing Penny

The Beauty of Love in Those We Shame

Little Kitty Goes to School

Broken before the Storm

The Special Little Sister

The Better Betty

Friendly Monsters: Behind the Computer

Making Dollars Make Sense: Business Ownership at any Age

Butter Me Fly: My Way Home

Inspirational Note!

Deeply motivating and highly inspiring, Broken before the Storm is an inspiring, powerful book that will rouse your inner warrior and also give you the courage and strength to weather the storms the world sends your way with all the stoicism of a veteran soldier.

In this powerful story of hope, Cheurlie Pierre-Russell chronicles the tribulations of Kourtney 'Jacobie' Rouchon and her struggles with muscular dystrophy.

This book is a mere hint of the of inspiration of Kourtney's life story.

I knew early on that I had to share Kourtney's purpose with the world, as I am honored to have been involved in supporting her during this difficult time. Her story is one of unwavering faith, the power of will and the refusal to give up and let go.

Unlike other kids, Kourtney has had to live this stark reality all her life and learn not only how to just cope with it, but how to excel and thrive despite it.

I hope you will enjoy reading about Miracle's life story.

Cheurlie Pierre-Russell

Publishing Information

Printed in the United States of America

All rights reserved. Except as permitted under the U.S. Copyright Act of 1976, no part of this publication may be reproduced, distributed or transmitted in any form or by any means, or stored in a database or retrieval system, without the prior written permission of the publisher.

This is a work of nonfiction. The names, dates, places, characters, and incidents are either the product of the author's imagination or are used fictitiously, and any resemblance to actual persons, living or dead, business establishments, events or locales is entirely coincidental and incidental to the real events in the time period the story is placed.

Copyright © 2018 by Cheurlie Pierre-Russell

All Rights Reserved

Cheurlie Pierre-Russell
Miami, Florida

Mommy's Little Miracle

*M*iracle hated to see other children staring at her. She hated it more than being on a nasty breathing machine that kept her on her bed for days and days at a time, or wearing her awkward, uncomfortable leg brace.

As a young girl, she already felt different from everyone else. She felt different because she had to depend on her wheelchair to move around. She was saddened by a disability that had come to destroy her happiness during the storm.

The storm was the emergency delivery that had taken place with the number of doctors and nurses by Miracle's side. The ugly and wicked storm lasted for about four hours before it eventually had calmed.
And once it had finally calmed down, Miracle had been put sound asleep.
The doctors then gathered around the bedside and told Miracle's mother that some children were born with a disability that tried to destroy them. Some disabilities would outshine, while others might take more of a task to overcome.

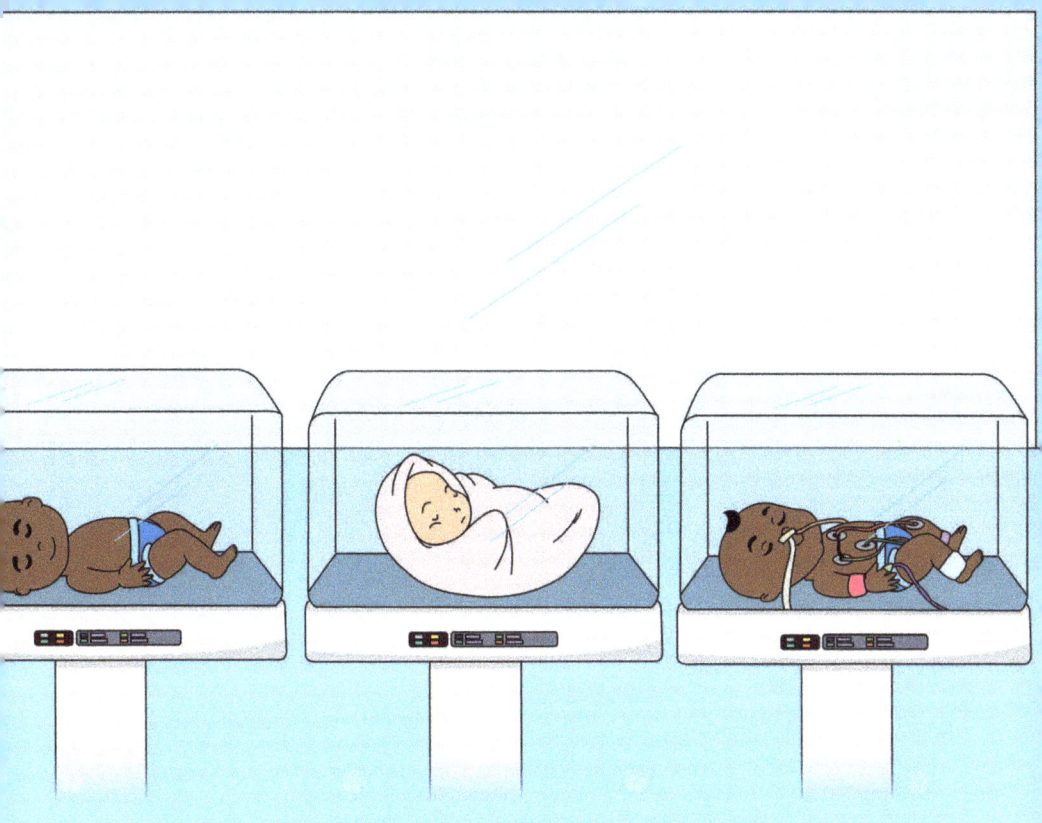

A Very Perfect Angel

Miracle was just as beautiful as she could be. She had a head full of black hair and had been born with ten fingers and ten toes on her little delicate body.

And with the baby being so adorable, Miracle's mother knew at this moment that her baby had been made perfectly for her. Although both of Miracle's hands were deformed and bent backward and her legs were stiffly straight, her mom loved every tiny and delicate bit of her sweet little baby girl.

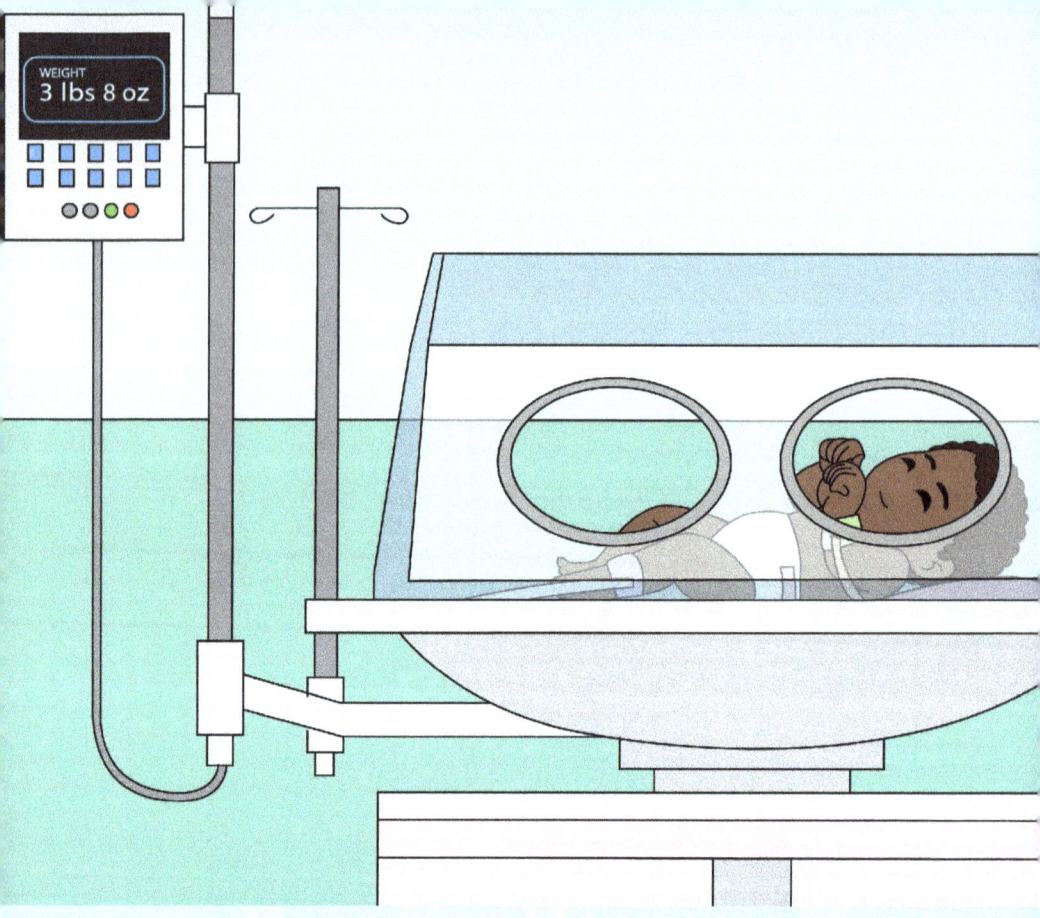

The truth was, Miracle could not possibly have been made into more of a tiny angel, not even if God had tried his very, very best to perfect her even more. It did not matter about all the things that people said were 'wrong' with the baby; what mattered were all the things that were right! And goodness me—there were way more of those than Miracle's mom could even count.

Miracle had been born weighing three pounds eight ounces and had to spend over eight months in the hospital. And, as is usually the way with little living things that are underweight, she had quite a few health problems. When a baby is born premature and below weight, then the first things that will suffer are the baby's little fragile lungs.

*D*uring her hospital stay, Miracle began having trouble breathing so they had to connect her delicate body to a breathing machine, and she stayed on it for the first few months of her life until her lungs were finally developed enough to breathe on their own. And that alone made Miracle wear her name with pride; not every little girl can even come through this struggle and breathe all on her own!

But now, there was a new problem. Miracle had cleared one huge hurdle only to run right into another!

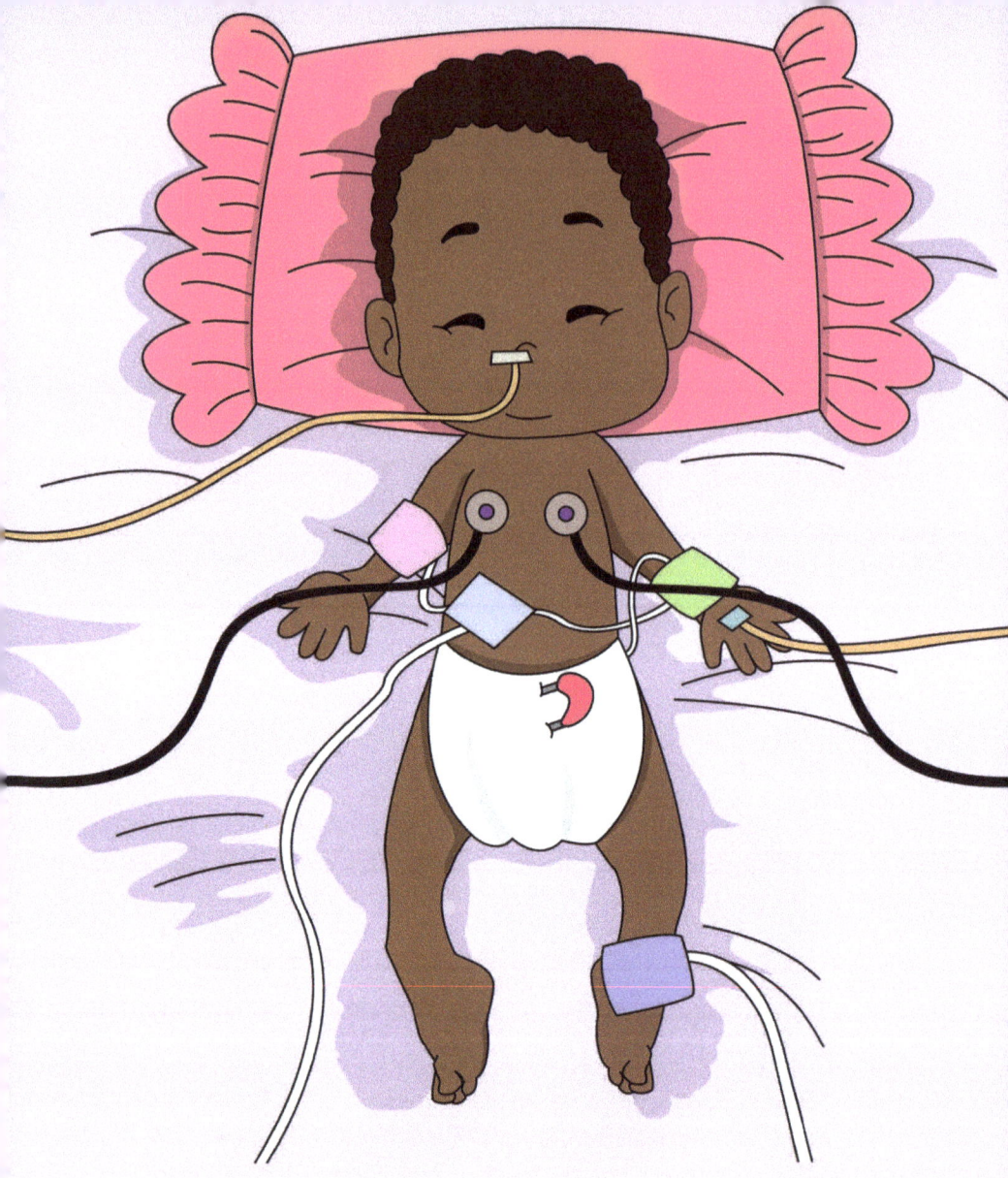

A New Fight

*N*ow, mommy's little Miracle wasn't able to be fed because she just didn't know how to use her jaws to suck.

"She can't latch on," the nurses said, looking disappointed and overwhelmed.

"No, such a fragile thing can't ever latch on. There's no chance."

No chance.

*M*iracle's mom was getting used to hearing these words. *Latching on* was when a little baby was able to suckle at its mother's breast, forming a nice firm contact with its lips so it could take its mother's milk, and then using its strong sucking power to draw down Mommy's milk. But a baby born tiny and under-developed would often have this struggle where it could not latch on in order to start sucking the milk. And even worse, a baby like this also couldn't even suck from the teat of a bottle. And this was Miracle. Everyone—all the doctors and nurses—crowded around the bed, looking upset and a little irritated, as if the baby was just not trying hard enough.

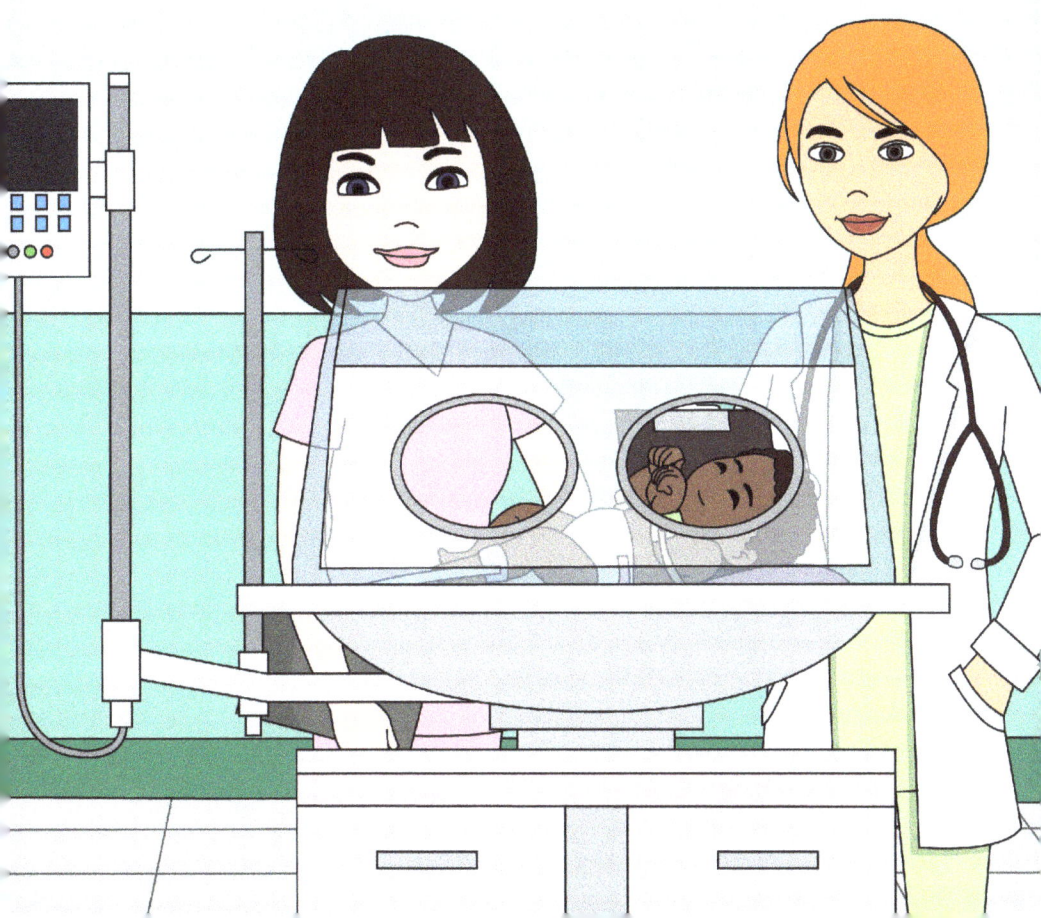

*M*iracle's mom just stood by too, looking on hopelessly, wishing, wishing, wishing…that they would stop talking about her perfect daughter as if she was an awful failure at everything.

It was difficult for her mother to watch her fight against the odds. The nurses had to feed her milk in a long tube through her nose, to ensure she was receiving the nutrients necessary to grow. The tube was hard and plastic and went right down from her tiny little nostrils deep into her belly, and a machine pushed the milk in now and then, making a terrible pumping sound—a scary sound that should never have to be heard when a baby feeds.

It must all have been so horribly uncomfortable, but little Miracle just put up with it.

And every so often, the baby would lock her beautiful gaze onto her mother's own eyes, as if to say: *see, I will be fine… you just keep on loving me, and I will show you what I can do. We will show all these people how wrong they are!*

Beating the Odds

So, even though she'd been born with a medical condition, Miracle was defeating her disabilities day by day. She was born so tiny her diapers fit her pink teddy bear with the black nose that lay beside her in her crib.

Miracle was a very tough and determined little fighter as she battled daily to make her body stronger.

*I*t was clearly understood by everyone in Miracle's circle that she was faced with major challenges. Nobody ever denied that; in fact, the doctors and nurses seemed to almost relish her struggles, always making things sound much worse than they eventually proved to be!

The family had faith in Miracle. If she came through her struggles, wonderful. If she didn't and was left with a problem or two, well, they knew all children were not born the same anyhow, and that this made every child uniquely beautiful in their own special way.

Miracle's mother told everyone in her circle to help support Miracle through their prayers. Her mother knew prayer was stronger than hope.

$\mathcal{T}$herefore, Pam posted a note above Miracle's crib that read:
   "*Life may seem cruel for the choices it makes—but the choices it makes are no mistakes.*"

Miracle's progress was a typical example of her being far from a mistake, and it sent a message to all the medical staff that Miracle was a gift from God.

Miracle's mother Pam and her Aunt Laura took lead to help her overcome her obstacles. They wanted her to continue fighting against her disability and all the separate problems that came along with it. Her mother knew she had to get her baby's hands fixed so that it would not delay her later in life.

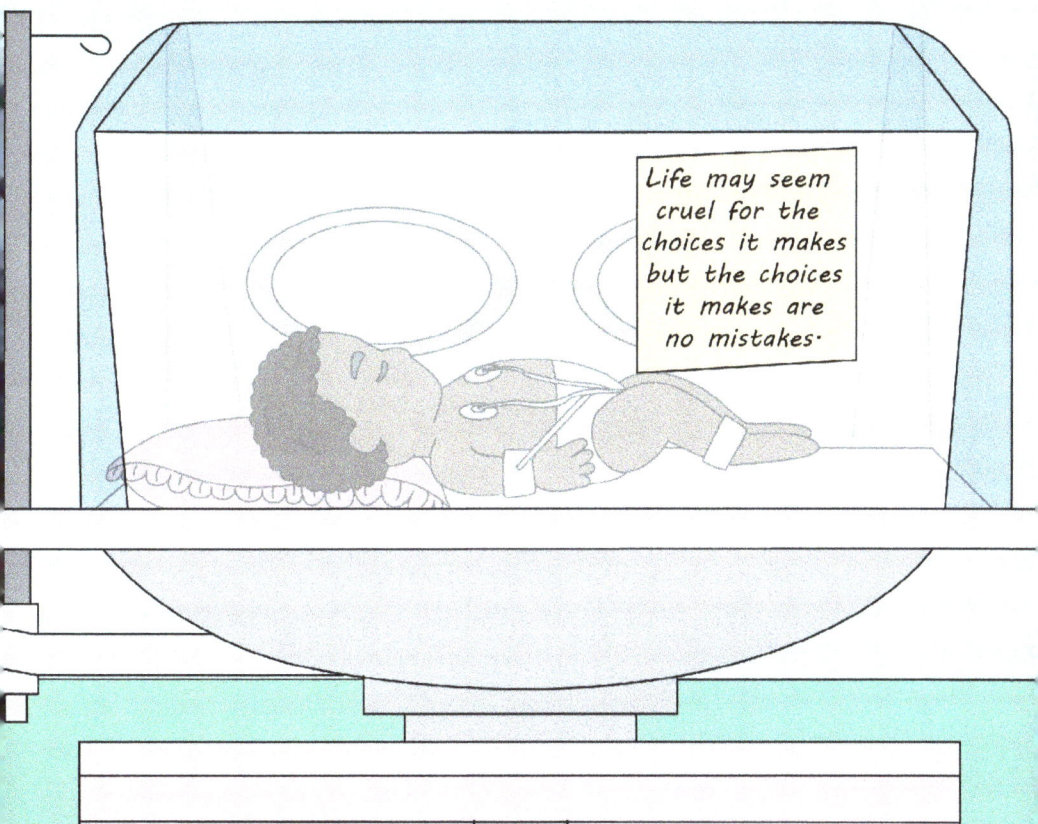

A Special Prayer

Miracle's mom took Miracle to see several doctors to determine if her hands could be put in a cast to straighten them. Pam knew Miracle would be able to enjoy life more and feel more comfortable amongst her friends if her hands were fixed.

Unfortunately, every doctor declined her request; they did not believe they could fix Miracle's hands because she was too young.

Mom was disappointed with every doctor's visit, so Pam and her sister Laura sat around the house devising a plan. Miracle's mother refused to give up because she was determined to have her daughter rise above that medical storm.

Pam had to visit one more doctor in hopes that he would cast Miracle's hands. Once again, she was turned away with disappointment. Pam walked out of the doctor's office and got down on her knees, right there in the corridor, and began praying.

Her prayer was asking God to help her remain focused on her daughter's condition, so it didn't interfere with Miracle's self-esteem.

Miracle's mother got up and slowly pushed the stroller out of the medical building and down the sidewalk while staring at the concrete ground. She realized something terrible in this moment. She saw how she was beginning to feel just like the doctors and nurses who seemed to abandon all hope in Miracle.

At this moment, she felt all hope was lost and nothing would come forth with her every attempt for Miracle to live a better life. With the dark clouds over her head, her mother could only hope a guardian angel was coming into Miracle's life

A Homemade Fix!

Aunt Laura witnessed her sister feeling extremely sad because no doctors wanted to help her daughter. Laura told Pam, "Let's go home. We will make Miracle her own homemade hand brace."

Laura stated she just needed two pieces of cardboard and some tape. Pam ran into the laundry room for a medium-sized cardboard box then hurried over to the kitchen and rummaged through the tool drawer for the tape.

They both got back on the floor with Miracle and began making their homemade hand brace for both of her hands. Pam held her hand straight as Laura took the piece of cardboard and laid it against Miracle's hand, while straightening her hand and tapping it firmly around.

Laura did this to both of Miracle's hands and told Pam to leave the cast on there for at least six months for the best results.

*N*either of them knew if it could work—but at least they could have some hope, something the doctors were not giving them.

Miracle's progress was quickly evident because she soon began reaching for her hanging mobiles that dangled above her car seat. Miracle was not even a year old and things were improving a great deal for her, in spite of everything and everyone!

This was a hard experience for Pam as a mother because she was the only parent present during this difficult time. She had never heard of this medical condition until Miracle had come into her life.

Pam had expected her daughter's arrival to be different from an emergency delivery where she found herself pleading for her daughter's life. On the other hand, witnessing her daughter's rapid progress brought her so much joy.

$\mathcal{M}$iracle's occupational therapy sessions with other children were like playdates for her. It allowed her to see and play with other children who were battling with other medical conditions. Miracle had a little setback, but her angel Aunt Laura had stepped in.

Aunt Laura had told Miracle's mother to leave the cast on the baby's hand for at least six months. So, there the braces remained as requested by her aunt. Anxious to remove the cast while eagerly wanting to see results, Pam struggled a little. But, in the end, she managed to leave the braces on for an extra month! It was such an achievement.

When Miracle turned seven months old, the homemade cast was removed. Life was beginning to blossom for Miracle.

Miracle's hand came out straight and normal; Mom could barely believe her own eyes!

Miraculous Moves

That was the beginning of Miracle's happiness and everyone was so happy for her. At that moment, her disability began to fade away because the light was shining on her hands. At that moment, she was able to hold her pacifier, bottle, and a spoon on her own.

Miracle began to make some miraculous moves with her hands. She began picking up her pacifier and putting it straight in her mouth. In fact, she was able to hold a small plastic bottle with no help. She continued to make progress using her now stronger hands. It had been a tough battle to watch her wearing casts for seven long months, but it had all been worthwhile

*P*am decided to educate herself more about her daughter's condition. She had also learned that all children suffering from muscular dystrophy suffered abnormal body temperature. Miracle's legs were always cold like ice when you touched them, while her forehead would be sweating. Her mother also found out muscular dystrophy led to weakness and loss of muscle strength in the lower part of the body.

So, Miracle's everyday job was to stand on her legs for as long as possible. She also had to constantly do leg exercises to get her legs stronger day by day. In addition, she had her supportive mother constantly encouraging her to overcome her medical illness.

Her mother continued to look for ways to help her gain muscle strength in her legs. Unlike other children her age, Miracle never learned how to walk. Miracle had to learn how to guide and balance herself with her leg brace on while using her crutches.

Miracle fell so frequently while trying to stand for long periods of time to strengthen her muscles. She broke her fragile leg bones every single time she fell. She did not give up as she had a strong supportive mother and family behind her. Being the smart little girl that she was, she realized life was easy for some children and very hard for others.

Learning to be 'Normal'

*M*iracle believed every child should get a chance to experience what being born normal felt like.

She felt life wasn't fair to children who got chosen randomly. Nonetheless, Miracle was being taught how to appreciate life.

Miracle had to learn how to "crawl" instead of walk. She would crawl by using her hands to move forward while her legs would lifelessly follow behind.

She had no feeling in her legs which made it difficult for her to walk, sit up straight, and crawl using her hands and feet.

Thankfully, after a couple of exercise sessions from her mother and aunt, she began making a lot of progress with her unique crawl. But even though she had progressed with her hands, her feet and back remained the same.

Miracle's disability caused her back to arch and curve outward, making her upper body lean completely forward.

Despite her fragile back and her lifeless legs, Miracle got potty-trained at three years old. She had to use her unique way of mobility to crawl her way to the bathroom.

Her mother did not make life any easier for Miracle.

After four months of potty training, Miracle was fully potty-trained wearing panties only, and no pull-ups.

The battle for help became more desperate as Pam was now requesting a body cast for her beautiful daughter, to help form her body in a straight position. She received excuses after excuses from the doctors. The doctors' denials led to yet more disappointment for Pam.

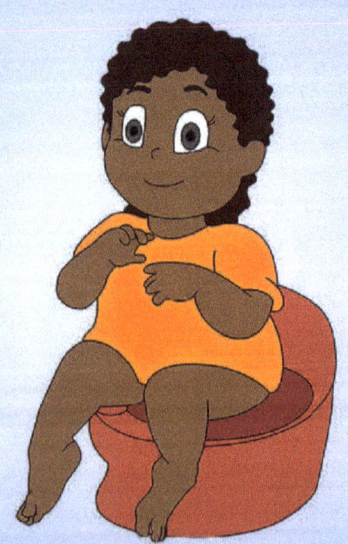

Putting up a Fight

Pam and Laura were willing to put up a battle for Miracle to overcome this part of her disability. So, they teamed up and went ahead and created a cardboard body cast for Miracle.

Her homemade body cast was not holding strong because the cardboard was too weak for the process. They both tried to use some creativity in the process, but all odds were against them. It was clear they needed something stronger, like a piece of plywood or board.

Aunt Laura eagerly left the house to go and purchase the plywood board at the nearest hardware store. She had the pieces cut out to fit Miracle's back from her neck to her buttocks. They attempted to strap her down on the wood but noticed it was hurting her because she began crying. They knew forcing it would probably cause unintentional damage to her back or worsen her disability. So, they abandoned this idea.

A New Wheelchair!

At her four-year-old birthday party, her mother rolled in her new pink wheelchair. Everyone cheered in excitement at the beautiful gem that was making amazing moves. Miracle's amazing progress kept defeating the storm.

Her family realized the easiest part of Miracle's life was when everyone would get together to encourage Miracle during her progress.

Pam did not want her daughter to think that the storm was over; there were going to be many more challenges in life she would have to face. Another victory Miracle overcame, only meant she would move onto the next challenge to follow.

Having to come so far, she now had to learn how to ride and control her wheelchair at four years old.

Despite Miracle having had over a hundred doctor's visits, being hospitalized more than five times, and having to wear a homemade hand cast for seven long months, her inner light was beginning to brighten. Miracle knew there was no reason for her to give up now. Miracle was ready to take on what her peers were doing so she could conveniently go into her next chapter of life

*H*er mother had to take both Miracle and the wheelchair to Miracle's physical therapist in order to teach her how to use it. Miracle knew once she understood how to control her wheelchair, she would be able to move freely with the other children in her family. Imagine her knowing that she would be able to play with her peers by moving around and not be stuck in one place!

Miracle learned how to run, stop, turn right and turn left in her new wheelchair. She was now very independent and could be her own person, going pretty much wherever she wanted, and nothing was going to stop her! Best of all, nobody now told her all the things she could *not* do! Now, they said, *I can't believe you can do all that!*

Miracle's Graduation

The fragile, beautiful girl who'd had to face such a medical storm had now graduated from high school at the age of eighteen. She made her entire family proud, graduating from high school.

During her high school graduation speech, she said to the entire audience, "I overcame the hardest storm in life and that was to be born with muscular dystrophy. Nothing else in life can be more difficult for me. I am known as the 'Disabled Girl' who did not let my medical condition control my purpose in life. So, where exactly is the disability?"

Everyone cheered and applauded. Indeed; where was Miracle's disability now? Where had it disappeared to? All anyone could see was the girl's abilities. The *'dis'* had buried itself away, hanging its head in shame. And Pam thought how this should be a lesson for all kids, not to give in to all the things they were told they could not manage to do.

At that very moment, Pam knew from the day Miracle was born that she had done a superb job building Miracle's self-esteem. Pam had also done everything in her power to help Miracle grow and progress with kids in her age group. Her efforts had even been more paramount, considering her daughter was said to be 'disabled'.

Miracle's story is a true inspiration. Her disability was explained to her mother and she just took the bull by the horns and made sure it was dealt with accordingly. She never let anyone tell her things were impossible.

As Pam mentioned, with a team of supporters, prayer, and faith, all disabled children can overcome their disabilities. With small or little efforts and failures along the way, success can—and will—be achieved.

BROKEN BEFORE THE STORM

Every person who comes into life has some kind of trial to battle during their storm of life.

Broken before the Storm follows the true story of Miracle, also known as Kourtney—her real name—who was born fragile at birth. With a medical disability called muscular dystrophy and when others didn't believe she could rise above her storm, her mother and aunt showed Miracle just what she had the potential to become if she never lost hope and kept trying

C. PIERRE-RUSSELL

 was born and raised in sunny Miami, FL, it was natural for Cheurlie Pierre-Russell to join the United States Navy. Her high point came during Operation Uphold Democracy on the island nation of Haiti, where she worked as a translator. Leaving the Navy was difficult but it was time to start a family and tackle a new career.

C. Pierre-Russell graduated from Georgia State University with a Bachelor of Arts in Sociology, later earning a Master of Science in Psychology from Walden University.

Her desire to strive in education led her to study the development and perception of children's lives through the influence of social context, and she has also studied children's intellectual development.

These combined areas of interest influenced her to write children's books, to help them understand their own cognitive way of life.

A strong role model for women and children, C. Pierre-Russell is a wife and has three amazing children of her own.

Now, she writes both fiction and non-fiction for kids of all ages, covering many subjects.

C. Pierre-Russell feels every child is a future leader and deserves only the best!

> To find out about C. Pierre-Russell's next book release,
> visit her Instagram page: https://www.instagram.com/j3russellbook/
> or her Facebook page: https://www.facebook.com/

Kourtney 'Jacobie' Rouchon

www.ingramcontent.com/pod-product-compliance
Lightning Source LLC
Chambersburg PA
CBHW051604010526
44118CB00023B/2813